Just Kidding

poems by

Dion Farquhar

Finishing Line Press
Georgetown, Kentucky

Just Kidding

For Alex and Matt

who re-affirmed in countless ways what I struggled to

learn through books—that where there are two, one

does not have to be superior and the other inferior

Copyright © 2018 by Dion N. Farquhar
ISBN 978-1-63534-534-6 First Edition
All rights reserved under International and Pan-American Copyright Conventions. No part of this book may be reproduced in any manner whatsoever without written permission from the publisher, except in the case of brief quotations embodied in critical articles and reviews.

ACKNOWLEDGMENTS

Two – *Wonderful Terrible* (Main Street Rag Publishing, 2013)
The Kiss – *phren-Z* (December 2015)
Fraternity – *Monterey Bay Poetry Anthology* (2004); *Feet First* (Evening Street Press, 2010)
Four – *The Birds We Piled Loosely* – April/May 2016
Candy – *Porter Gulch Review* (Spring 2006); *Feet First* (Evening Street Press, 2010)
Riding the Q Train – *phren-Z* (December 2015)
Dinner on September 11th with Eight Year Olds – *Columbia Poetry Review* (Spring 2015)
Food Factor – *Perigee* 3:2 (2005); *Feet First* (Evening Street Press, 2010); *Wonderful Terrible* (Main Street Rag Publishing, 2013)
Always Problems – *To Topos* (2008); and in *Cleaving* (Poets Corner Press, 2007); *Feet First* (Evening Street Press, 2010)
Vocabulary Drill – *Cleaving* (Chapbook: Poets Corner Press, 2007)
Things Not To Write About – *phren-Z* (December 2015)

Publisher: Leah Maines
Editor: Christen Kincaid
Cover Art: Alexander Farquhar-Leicester
Author Photo: "Author photos coached by Paula Gould, Amy Mintzer, and Matt Farquhar-Leicester."
Cover Design: Elizabeth Maines McCleavy

Printed in the USA on acid-free paper.
Order online: www.finishinglinepress.com

Author inquiries and mail orders:
Finishing Line Press
P. O. Box 1626
Georgetown, Kentucky 40324
U. S. A.

Table of Contents

Thirty-nine Weeks at 46 1

Use Your Words 4

Two 5

Age of Reason: 27 Months 6

The Kiss 8

Fraternity 9

Four 11

Candy: a History 12

Sheltered 14

Riding the Q Train 15

Dinner on September 11th with Eight-Year-Olds 16

Food Factor 17

The Abu Graib of Childhood 19

Rocky 20

Ten Rules for Ten Year Olds 22

Always Problems 23

Criminals 25

Vocabulary Drill 28

Countdown Year 30

The Night Before 32

Things Not To Write About 33

Thirty-nine Weeks at 46

An I.V. in your arm, two round disks belted
to your bloated belly, which they make you keep to bed,
no new-age frills: tubs or rocking chairs, birthing stools
for you, high-risk *elderly prima gravida.*

Persistent, though no spring chicken,
you grew these babes from donor eggs
plucked from a 25-year-old, into fourteen
pounds of babies, now breaking your back.

You'd like to walk around, you say,
though terrified, to get this labor going.
But you've got to stay put,
The twin monitor isn't portable.

Hours of heartbeats scratch onto tapes,
snake in folds to the floor. A stream
of nurses in and out, pass yards
of paper strips from hand to hand,

scan the squiggles, throw small smiles
leaving you, unsure of what to think or feel,
along with your reading partner, to the machine's hum.
Coated paper readouts rustle on their piles.

Until the nagging beep began. Baby A's
heartbeat slows to eighty. Your doctor rushes
in to read the strip. *You know what
this means?* she says. *Yes, when?*

As soon as I can put a team together.

Time speeds up, fast forward from
now on. Another nurse comes in
with tubes in plastic packets.

A catheter to catch your urine.

Next, they want to wrest your wedding ring
worn on your pinky because your ring finger
got so fat. You refuse, so they back down

and stretch a piece of sterile tape over it.
You are rolled into a ball, your spine
swabbed with alcohol for the needle
that would make you pain-free for days.

Minutes later you try to lift your legs,
wriggle your toes. You feel nothing
but dead weight from breastbone down.
You turn to the anesthesiologist,

This is what paraplegics feel like, isn't it?
Yes, he says, smiling. *Where's Marsh?*
you ask, as they rush your gurney down a hall.
You turn your head to see him running
to catch up, pulling a green cap on,
blue eyes and glasses peeking over the paper mask
Do you have music? the OB asks. Marsh hands her

our Vivaldi CD, and you hear music
cleave the techno-chatter of the team
huddled by your feet. The autofocus swinging from his neck
Marsh tells you, even-voiced:

> They're gutting you open,
> Click, oh my god, click
> they're lifting one out,
> click, they've got him...

Wah, Wah, Wah

You hear, like in the movies, a baby
crying, loud and clear. Wah, wah, wah.
Half the team rushes over to one corner

of the room and Marsh goes on:

> They're going in for the other one.
> Click. I see feet, legs, toochas, click
> (the bugger was breech).
> they're pulling him out, click…

More loud squawky crying. It feels like
forever before they bring you a baby
cap pulled down, bundled up, only a tiny wrinkly face,
eyes shut tight. You hold him close, a cuddle

high up on your chest,
where there's still some feeling
You don't know what
to tell this tiny thing

your first-born son, the culture calls it, but only
by a minute. You look over at your husband,
who's bursting with something, clutch in your chest
and you feel a sting in the eye, a catch in the throat.

> *Hello, little one. Welcome.*

A pause and they bring
the other one, Baby B,
and you just can't believe it,
but you greet him too.

> *Hi there, little one. Hello.*

Then you wait for them to sew you up,
slower than slicing through seven layers of muscle.
The babies triple their lifespan with their father
in the nursery while you lie there, eager
to get back to him and them, impatient

Use Your Words

The usual 6 a.m. charge into our bedroom
squealing with delight,
—instead of jumping on us—
head straight for the bookcases

begin pulling books down,
off the lower shelves,
        bolting up, our eyes lock:
        Could this be the terrible twos
        starting early, at 18 months

Mobile, but not rational,
the pediatrician sighs,
as they grab at the
blood pressure cuff
dangling from her wall

You're in for some
challenging times,
she says,
twin boys are tough.

Ambivalent
about authority
and order, ourselves,
we're late
in child-gating the house

Next, they start
noticing each other:
biting, tackling, hitting
wrestling, pulling hair
strong and fast, equally matched

We separate them,
blessed anarchy
staunched for an instant

Two

What's your name?
Alex
You're Alex.
What's your name?
Name. Grin.
What's my name?
Mommy. Proud.
Yes. *Your* name is Alex.
Alex.
What's your name?
Mine. Name.
Yes. Your name.
Mine.

Age of Reason: 27 Months

Saturday night, friends over for dinner
just sitting down to eat
when Alex woke up and cried,
Book. Book, Mommy!

"It's dark, sweetie.
It's night-night."
Book, book, he insisted.
I got him a book,
which he clutched to his chest,
Read, Mommy, read.
Taking a deep breath,
I sat down and held the book
out toward him
so he could see the pictures.

*Once upon a time,
there was a little boy
who wouldn't go night-night
even though it was very late.
He called for his mommy
and asked her to read him a story,
and the mommy said,*
Little Boy, it's too dark for stories.
We'll read in the morning.

*But the boy insisted,
so his mommy began to tell him
a story. She told him that
she and daddy were
on a playdate and their friends.
were waiting for her.*
"Why," the boy asked.
*Because adults play by just
sitting still and talking.*
This must have sounded very boring
because his head

nestled onto the pillow

he'd fallen asleep.
Tiptoeing out of the room,
I got to the door when
his twin brother called,
Book, Mommy.
He held out the book
he'd taken to bed with him,
Story, Mommy, story.

The Kiss

I want a kiss

You just got a kiss.

I dint see the noise

        Another kiss,
loud smack of lips

        smiles

See, dat's de noise.

Fraternity

> *Freedom is a practice.*
> —*Foucault*

Thought I knew something
about equality
(one of my passions)
but my twin sons
teached me something new

Power is everywhere
        Not a trickle down
        but flash or strobe
& so is resistance

Take turns our mantra
useless as New Age
psychobabble

        Me first, meeeeee, meeeee, meeeee
        who has his seatbelt   unbuckled first
        who gets to open the house door
        at night, who gets to turn off the light
        who gets tucked in first

So we mark it on the calendar
lest we forget and be unfair
though it starts anew each day
        who gets his cereal milk poured first

milestones provoke bigger crises
        who the Tooth Fairy visited first
        who learned to tie his shoes first
        who made "strokes plus" first

        the saving grace, exogamy
        Matt loves Cookie (large elephant)
        and Cici (small elephant)
        Pinky (flamingo) and Cheesy (mouse)

        While Alex loves
Three Horn (stegosaurus)
Fishy (dolphin), Ralph (rabbit)
and Mickey (mouse)
Egg them on

Demanding goodnight kisses and hugs
First, first, first.
Meeeee. To be first. Always to be first.

We are saved by the fact
that one is crazy 'bout "speriments"
and any vehicle that moves
how everything works
or is put together

the other is a ham
nuts about dancing
& "making a show"
loves to draw pictures
already a media addict

        thank god they're fraternal.

Four

Tucking Alex in
after two books
still bright-eyed, not sleepy
looks at my chest

Can I see your nickels?
You mean 'nipples'?
Yes.
I pull my tee shirt up,
lift my bra over one breast.

He looks, pauses,
I was a tiny baby inside there.

Candy: a History

for Matt and Alex

Impossible to imagine life
radically other
futures not hemmed in by same
sons' asking, *Were there cars
when you were little, Dad?*

Yes, we had cars, motoring even
Dinah Shore belting,
See the USA in your Chevrolet
blowing a rousing sign-off kiss,
optimism in black-and-white
before Gameboy, PlayStation

How did we live? I'll tell you:

The candy was fabulous.
Something had to be.

No birthday parties for twenty
at climbing gyms, roller rinks,
or swimming pools, no endless bribes
and pay-offs—just several good smacks,
their mantra, *Don't talk back.*

Green and red sugar water
in tiny Coke-shaped wax bottles.
Break their tops off and suck them dry
till the paraffin flaked onto your lips.
Fancy candy cigarettes, hot pink for the flame
at one end, dark brown faux filter at the other.

We had Junior Mints and Sugar Daddies
Dots and Red Hots, Mr. Goodbar and Milky Ways
Baby Ruths and Snickers, Good and Plenty
Tutti Frutti, Life Savers and all the Ludens

mentholated cherry you could suck
in a morning of math

So shut your eyes tight, bite your tongue:

Imagine another world

where it's not stuck-in-the-sixties
to want more justice,
an end to sexism,
class, white supremacy.

I can't even subtract
all the tech, jet travel,
the Web, condo sprawl,
everywhere a mall
never a live voice operator

      I hate it and love it

          the difference   the same

                                    a future

Yes, there were cars.

Sheltered

I.   Spring, Kindergarten in Santa Cruz

Walking to school, Matty pauses
at the top of the stairway linking
our neighborhood to the school play yard,
points at a looming spire with a cross on it,
Mom, why is there a big "T"?
It's not a "T"; it's a cross.
I'll tell you more tonight.

II.   Christmas at the Met

Their favorite is the armor
especially the ones for dogs, horses, and boys
and the weapons: jewel-inlaid swords,
lances, elaborately-carved guns.
After the crèche on the main floor
(they know about the baby Jesus),
we climb the stairs, telling them
a lie: you have to walk through
rooms of painting to get to the armor
(it's really on the main floor
all the way to the right, past the pyramid)
and we're moving from one crowded room
of seventeenth-century crucifixions to the next
when Alex asks,

Why are they being so mean to that man?

The hushed hum of hundreds stops cold.
"That's Jesus dying on the cross."
*You mean this is the same guy
as the baby downstairs?*
Yes, but all grown up.

They shake their heads in disbelief.

Riding the Q Train at Six

to visit Jacob, their noses pressed
against the window of the lead car
to see every blue and red marker light,
the red-yellow-green signal stop lights,
exciting speed, sharp turns, screeching brakes
high-pitched whine of steel on steel,
kids riveted, the City's power
in your bones
the whole half hour ride.

As the train comes out of the ground
in Brooklyn, after Prospect Park,
I ask, "What do you see?"
and Alex says,
It's another world—
pretty houses and trees.

That's when I knew,
already a New York ex-pat

Dinner on September 11th with Eight-Year-Olds

The night of 9/11
we sat down to dinner

Alex:
*If I was on that plane
I would have punched
those hitch-hikers out*
making a fist with his hand
and hangs a punch in the air

Matt:
*It's good they hadn't served the food yet,
so after it crashed into the building
they could serve the people food
and then they wouldn't be hungry*

Food Factor

1.
For an arm and a leg
you can dine out:
>Insalata, primi and piatti

First a salad: *misticanza*
with shallot vinaigrette
focaccia croutons,
then scallops *en scapece*,
a sweet corn pancake
& spicy pepper relish.
Next, *gnocchi grattinati*
baked in a *wood* oven
winter squash, sage and prosciutto
topped with mozzarella and toasted walnuts

2.
The rest of us eat in,
stay home & cook:
I drizzle
sun-dried tomato *olio*
> from *Coeur d'Olive*
>> organic olive grower
>> four hours into the foothills

onto our arugula,
asking the boys

> for the third time
to turn off the TV
and come to the table.

Forego the next round
—Trauma Olympics
> for voyeurs,
the prize, a new car.

Grasped with the mouth

plucked off a table,
live spiders
        African cave-dwellers
       big as crabs:
winner ate 12.

The Abu Graib of Childhood

Pick up your toys.

Dirty clothes go in the laundry basket.

I didn't hear "please."

Ask to be excused from the table.

Bring your plate to the sink.

Put your homework in your backpack.

Rocky

> *There's a special providence in the fall of a sparrow. If it be now,'tis not to come; if it be not to come, it will be now; if it be not now, yet it will come: the readiness is all. Since no man has aught of what he leaves, what is't to leave betimes?*
> —*Hamlet*

Six years he spent with us,
never knew how old he was,
adopted from the SPCA,
—we went in for a dog
came out with a bird—
never sick a day, Rocky
loved to sing, most of all he loved
hubbub and the sound of running
water—same jittery dance, head
bobbing left, right, across his perch.

Then one morning, we found him
dead, eyes frozen open,
lying stiff on the floor of his cage.
Alex remembered what his friend
Anna did when she found her budgie
dead—she wrapped him in a Ziploc,
put him in the freezer so after
school, she could bury him.

So Alex picked Rocky up with
a paper towel and put him in
a baggie. When he came home from
school he went right to the garden
dug a hole by himself, refused
help, but told us to stay, then
called his brother to come.
He handed round a piece of paper.

Read it to yourself, he said, handing
it first to mom. The writing told
how great his bird had been,
how much he had been loved,

how we'd always miss him,
then squatted down, and gently slipped
his body from the plastic bag
laid it in the dirt and placed the folded
paper over it, stood up and
shoveled some dirt into the hole,
handed it to his brother with
a look that said, *Join me. Help.*
Then dad and mom. More patting
the soil down, carefully.
Then Alex looked up, said,
Rocky and the words
will help the flowers bloom.

Ten Rules for Ten Year Olds

I. Bottom Line

1. Wear helmets when biking or skateboarding

2. No jumping over furniture

3. Eat only at table or counter

4. No using stove, sharp knives, or tools without adult present

5. No coming in and out through windows

6. No lighting candles

II. Nice

1. No screaming

2. Answer when called the first time

II. Extra Nice

1. Sharing with your brother

2. Saying *please* and *thank you*

Always Problems

Only the genius of Disney
enchanted kingdom,
hydraulics, gears
the teeth of a machine
a people primed
for enchantment
could have us believe:
our Santa, our star,
every girl a princess
good triumphing over evil,
world without change
seamless same.

My twelve-year old
techie has no idea
though *his* Disney
be mixed
with dead rappers
and X-box.
How I wish it were the X
as in Malcolm
though that association's
almost impossible
for a relatively privileged
twelve-year-old white boy
who's OK with killing
in video self-defense
his Bond a good guy
Brit operative
sort of like us
rooting out
militants
newspeak calls them

it takes a vacuum
socialism   atavism
chronic insomnia

    The base you always have with you.

Criminals

1.   The Bust

Your husband's turn to pick them up.
Forty-five minutes pass.
He doesn't return.
The phone rings.

You need to come to school.
The kids are in the principal's office.
What happened?
It's not clear. They're all right.

You rush over to the junior high,
two squad cars parked outside.
One's in the principal's office, door closed.
Other's looking scared, trying not to cry

Your husband's there, pinched look,
says in a hushed voice:
They brought marijuana to school.
Two other boys are involved.

The door opens,
your other son comes out, head down.
The principal beckons you
and your husband to come in.

Four boys are involved,
They acted as a team.
The idea was to trade
a joint for a condom.

One had the hollowed-out book,
one the joint
a third the lighter,
and the fourth, the condom.
When I asked them

where they got the joint,
Matt said,
"From my Mom's stash."

    What snoops!
    It was in a jar
    inside a paper bag,
    in the back of my underwear drawer.

I'm wondering if you have
a medical marijuana card.

    No, but I can get one by tomorrow.

You understand,
when it comes to drugs
or violence, the schools
are very concerned.

    Oh, yes.

The thing is, one denied
being involved at all.
The lying is troublesome.
For now, they're both suspended for two days.

My husband and I look at each other.

Later, they'll have to go
to a hearing at
Juvenile Hall,
do community service.

    2.   The Confession

Many hours after

the silent ride home
and an unusually quiet dinner,
they did their homework

on the cleared table,
then asked politely
if they could watch TV.
  What do you think?

Bedtime came and went
without much comment.

I bit my lip.
Told them I loved them,

The one who denied
he was part of it
woke us up at 2,
came into our room, crying.

It was my idea.
I found the joint in your drawer
and made the plan.
I'm sorry.

Vocabulary Drill

for Jean, confrere

If I had a blog, I'd write about how you
don't have to get past the C's
of the 8th Grade National
Standards Vocabulary List
to smell language charring
on the spit of bellicosity,
scare quotes framing "education,"
leading down the primrose mine field,
but back to my story, I do digress.

There's *aide*, that proto-archaic
denominator with the *de camp* stripped out,
and *ambassador*, messenger of empire,
while *amphibious* and *armament* curtsey
to the technological prowess of Greek
and Latin roots, meanwhile *aristocrat's*
an eighth-grade word because class,
like the dinosaur, is extinct,
the old days bolder than ever
via *ballast* in animé.

Barbarian the unspeakable trace
—Babylon gave us banking and language—
the verb *besiege*, the noun *battalion*,
redeemed by *bravery*, counted by *brigade*
where wild and culture blend in *camouflage*,
a globe *careening* into this sorry state
that would *catapult* weaponry, require
classification to invent *cavalry*,
and that tragic niche, *civilian*, normalized

a column after the euphemism,
casualty, then *chaplain*, to bless each war,
a *computer* for *coordination*,
confederate to know the difference,

corrupt convoy of *corporation
counterfeiting consolation,*
each its rank-and-file niche.

Countdown Year

The year before
the nest empties
I'm already worried:
What I will do without them?

without

peanut butter jars rolling under beds
driving everywhere:
Jazz Band at 7 a.m.
Leadership Club
      whose movie nights get out at midnight
border-to-border college visits (California)
speech therapist
      (communication facilitator)
radio control flyers' club first Saturdays
family therapist (*Brain development is on your side.*)
Honor Band rehearsals two counties away
pediatric dentist, prescribing psychiatrist
trumpet lessons, orthodontist
Teen Aviators once a month at local airport
art lessons producing paintings
I'm not allowed to see (*Wait in the parking lot.*)
TB test at the country building
      (for summer day camp job)
cupcakes for forty, requested at 9 p.m.
Parent Board meetings that go til ten
admissions essays
tux rentals for prom, girls' corsages
Youth Symphony practice on Sundays
haircuts by the woman who works only on Saturdays
Winter Concert, Spring Concert
math tutor, tae kwon do
driving lessons, license test
Grad Day Planning meetings
Band Awards Night pot luck
school parent newsletter editing

unable to remember
who was captor/captive

The Night Before

the eight-hour drive to his freshman dorm
finally packed, at 2 a.m.
holds out two worn, folded pieces of paper

What should I do with Emma's letters?
sent from her diabetes' camp beyond cell range
I'd keep them and file them.

You've always filed everything important for me.
I run upstairs and grab a bunch of file folders.

Well now you have to do your own filing.
He looks puzzled.
You need to label each folder.

He writes a capital "E" on a tab,
unfolds the letters, gently presses out the creases
puts them in the folder, holds it up.

That's it. You got it.

Things Not To Write About

How each birthday, ever hopeful,
You'd think, maybe this year, it will get easier.

Wondering why you ever wanted to have a child

All the desperation, hurt, and anger they evoked

The emotional morass of the family

The day you told the family therapist in tears
I can't take it any more

The time one of them hit me and I threatened
to call the cops and have him sent to Juvenile Hall,
he grabbed the phone, waved it in my face,
saying, "Go ahead, I'll dial it for you."

The times I was in such a rage that I slapped one of them

The endless no-win flawed and awkward ricochet

Dion Farquhar is a poet and fiction writer with recent poems in *Mortar, Lady Blue, Birds Piled Loosely, Otoliths, Unbroken, Futures Trading, Local Nomad, Columbia Poetry Review, Shampoo, moria, BlazeVOX*, etc. Her first chapbook appeared with Poets Corner Press in 2007, and her first poetry book was published by Evening Street Press in 2010. Her second poetry book *Wonderful Terrible* was published in 2013 by Main Street Rag Publishing Company, and her second chapbook *Snap* was published by Crisis Chronicles Press in 2017. *Just Kidding* is her third chapbook. Unwilling to leave New York for work, in mid-life, she did leave her city for love, immigrating to Santa Cruz, where she lives with her partner and their twin sons (when home), missing her old friends and family in Manhattan, Brooklyn, and Connecticut, but enjoys a few friends and cousins in the Bay Area. She works as an exploited adjunct at two universities, teaching mostly composition but remains totally in love with, and committed to, the classroom and what can go on there. When she has a minute, she reads, writes, studies music, and is a Union activist.

www.ingramcontent.com/pod-product-compliance
Lightning Source LLC
LaVergne TN
LVHW041601070426
835507LV00011B/1244